Table of Cont

Can You Find These Words?

cooking

family

laughing

pet

I See Love

pet

I see love in my **pet.**

I see love in **laughing.**

I see love in **cooking**.

cooking

I see love in celebrations.

I see love in helping.

I see love in **family.**

family

Photo Glossary

 **cooking** (kuk-ing): Preparing and heating food for eating.

 **family** (FAM-uh-lee): A group of people related to one another.

 **laughing** (laf-ing): Making sounds and moving your face and body in a way that shows you think something is funny.

 **pet** (pet): A tame animal kept for company and treated with affection.

About the Authors/Photographers

 Kaitlyn Duling is a writer and editor who lives in Washington, DC. She believes that love can change the world! Kaitlyn loves traveling with her wife and trying new things.

 Martin Wong is a writer who lives in Los Angeles, California. He sees love in family and friends, future family and friends, and community.

 Alma Patricia Ramirez is a writer who enjoys writing in English and Spanish for children and adults. She finds love in knitting blankets for the family, playing with a puppy, and doing family activities, like playing games, baking, playing sports, and music.

 Allen R. Wells is a writer and mechanical engineer in Atlanta, GA. He loves to read and write and is happy that he's able to share his love for reading with children.

www.rourkeeducationalmedia.com

PHOTO CREDITS: cover: (background) ©Getty Images; cover, page 2, 4, 5, 10, 11, 14, 15: Kaitlyn Duling; page 2, 6, 7, 14, 15: Martin Wong; page 2, 3, 12, 13, 14, 15: Alma Patricia Ramirez; page 8, 9, 15: Allen R. Wells

Edited by: Hailey Scragg
Cover and interior design by: Lynne Schwaner

Library of Congress PCN Data
I See Love/ Kaitlyn Duling, Allen R. Wells, Martin Wong, Alma Patricia Ramirez
(Life Through My Lens)
ISBN 978-1-73165-186-0 (hard cover)(alk. paper)
ISBN 978-1-73165-231-7 (soft cover)
ISBN 978-1-73165-201-0 (E-book)
ISBN 978-1-73165-216-4 (e-Pub)

Library of Congress Control Number: 2021944579

Printed in the United States of America
01-3402111937